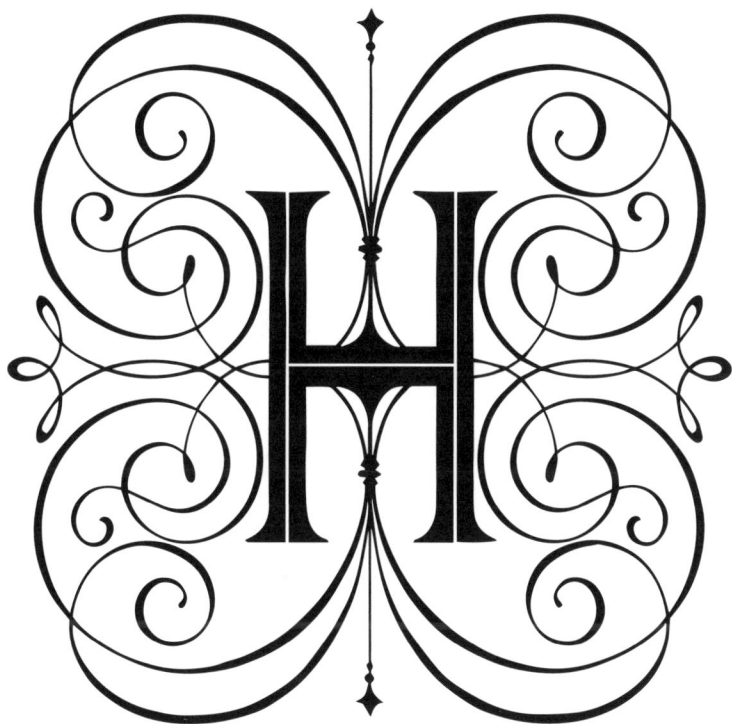

HANDSTYLE LETTERING
FROM CALLIGRAPHY TO TYPOGRAPHY

Published and distributed by
viction:workshop ltd.

viction:ary™

viction:workshop ltd.
Unit C, 7/F, Seabright Plaza, 9-23 Shell Street,
North Point, Hong Kong
Url: www.victionary.com   Email: we@victionary.com
 @victionworkshop
 @victionary_
 @victionworkshop

Edited and produced by viction:ary

Concepts & art direction by Victor Cheung
Book design by viction:workshop ltd.
Cover artworks by Adrian Iorga, Andreas Pedersen, Copenhagen Signs,
David Sanden, Novia Jonatan & Olga Vasik
Imprint image by Novia Jonatan
Foreword by Mike Meyer & Glenn Wolk

Second Edition
©2017, 2018, 2022 viction:workshop ltd.
Copyright on published work is held by respective designers
and contributors.

ISBN 978-988-75665-4-0
Printed and bound in China

I WAS NO DIFFERENT
TO ANY OTHER

SIGN
PAINTERS

IN THE MID-80's
who REFUSED to
SUCCUMB
TO THE "DREADED COMPUTER"
— AND LATER —
Understood
THAT IT WAS MERELY
TOOL!

Short, simple, getting the message across and to the point — the logic I apply to my sign designs is also used here as I write this foreword. My obsession with lettering began as a young boy when I hang out in my father's barbershop in a very small Midwestern American town, where I still operate and run my own sign shop. Lettering to me has been the ultimate escape to satisfaction and happiness. It still is, and always will be. It has taken me many, many years to acquire the technique but I know I can never get to master it all, and that's the beauty of it — knowing there is always another way to paint, or seeing hand-lettering right around the corner.

As I grow older, I realise what teaching means as a gift of giving, which was "tough love" to me in my early days. The repeated exhortations such as "you'd better get on it or you'll never be any good!" added grit and determination to my efforts to improve my art as an apprentice for six years. All I had in mind by that time was "I'll show you!"

I attended a small vo-tech school to learn about sign painting and lettering, and worked in two sign shops to receive training within a formal work environment. I remember how I always pestered the "old-school" painters who eventually became good friends of mine. I was no different to any other sign painters in the mid-80s who refused to succumb to the dreaded computer and later understood that it was merely a tool, much the same as my scroll saw or hammer are to me. It helped me make money, the root of all evil, and brought me happiness. It still does.

Lettering means even more as I started holding sign painting workshops in 2013. I like to let students learn by demonstrating what I was taught. Seeing me make mistakes is just as important as succeeding in drawing beautiful strokes. As my workshops brought me to different big cities, I noticed interests for lettering always come from the cutting edge of society and the younger generation. I've also learnt from my students that there are many other related trades where you can draw and be creative, such as graffiti, tattooing and graphic design.

Learning sign painting today is different from the old days only in the speed you can gather and send information. You still have to spend the same amount of time to put it into practice. Time investment is a major factor, or you may say the ultimate "shortcut" to learn lettering. Observe what's around you, take them all in, gather interesting examples that you find inspiring and surround yourself with great things, great lettering, family, and friends. (Consider chocolate, ice hockey and Studebaker trucks too!).

WE CRAVE THE HUMAN TOUCH – PERFECTION IN IMPERFECTION. FROM THE HAND RENDERED TYPE OF THE ILLUMINATED MANUSCRIPTS TO GUTTENBERG'S LETTERPRESS NO PAGE WAS EVER EXACTLY THE SAME

GLENN WOLK

Graphic designer

There is a human, timeless element to hand-lettering. It suggests craft over machine. Every day we are relentlessly bombarded by the media that not only stress conformity but also deliver messages in impersonal computer graphics. The advent of modern commercial printing ushered printing uniformity.

Luckily not all is lost, as there has been growing appreciation towards hand-rendered lettering in the graphic art world. We crave the human touch — perfection in imperfection. From the hand-rendered type of the illuminated manuscripts to Guttenberg's letterpress, no page was ever exactly the same.

With the introduction of Apple's Macintosh computer in the 1980s and its user-friendly interface, thousands of typefaces became readily available. Initially there was an infatuation with the computer as a one-stop shop for readymade types, layout and artwork. But a revolt against the clean lines and hard edges of digital typography followed, with a new crop of designers escaping their computer screens to paint letters and signs in the last decade, taking reference from designs made in as far back as the 19th century.

The shackles imposed by over dependence on computers broke as a whole new world of hand-lettered typography arose. Virtually the movement towards hand-drawn types occurs in all forms of visual communication, especially in advertising, book covers, posters, signage, product packaging and brand labels.

Working by hand has opened up the possibilities of reviving the aesthetics from the past. Some designers harken back to the 19th and 20th centuries and recreate type forms reminiscent of Art Nouveau and Art Deco designs. The work of Henri de Toulouse-Lautrec, Aubrey Beardsley, Alphonse Mucha and Gustav Klimt are certainly among the list. There is a strong presence of Cassandre, Bauhaus and Russian Constructivism too. Other artists may feel inspired by typography from the 1940s or 1950s, using influences of commercial artists such as Alex Steinweiss. For me, I prefer to mix lettering styles of different eras. With a little inspiration and playfulness, quoting from multiple sources allows me to create a new mixed vernacular.

Just because we crave for human touches and perfection in imperfection does not mean computers have no place in handmade type. Many lettering artists like me still start by drafting on the computer, then print it as a guide for detailing, and eventually scan and digitise the finished work back on the computer. I embrace this interplay between technology and crafts as a dance of sorts. Ultimately, in an internet-dominated age where the digital is a given, all work require computer systems to aid in the optimisation and reproduction of deliverables in bits and pixels.

In a world that has become increasingly standardised, hand-lettering fosters a sense of naturalism and individuality, like human beings in a society. The spaces between the letters are uneven and imperfect like nature. Lines are not straight and edges fade into one another, just like the world around us.

NOT FOR SELF

RATSCAVE

SFZ

SILVER LIGHT

TO BE is TO DO

CARPENTER

ONE LOVE

The road map to your special day, 2016.

Chalk on blackboard. Mural inspired by Monopoly to portray the bride and groom's wedding planning journey. Commissioned by Plan-Do-See Inc. Photo by Studio Harvest.

CHALKBOY

Hiroshima, Japan
IG:chalkboy.me / FB:CHALKBOY.ME

What began as a 30-minute café menu drawing routine had turned into a full-blown artistic career. Armed with his signature illustration-fused designs, CHALKBOY now travels the world to draw for shops, cafés and events.

How did you become a letterer? Do you see yourself more as a designer or a calligrapher?

The café in which I worked used to give every staff member up to 30 minutes each day to rewrite the chalkboard menu. Wanting to avoid going back to my shift, I always utilised the time to draw not only the menu but also beer and wine labels and whatnots, which started to attract attention and eventually became my "job". I see myself as a designer who draws "unskilled letters" and "undesigned fonts. For me it's more about having the right font in the right place with illustrations and ornaments than drawing beautiful characters, so that I convey the right message as a whole.

What's your creative style?

I improvise on the spot. When I create, I study the light, as well as people's movements and sight lines when visiting the actual site. Knowing what the client wants is also crucial.

What role does hand-lettering play in different areas of our visual world today?

I think handwritten letters convey way more information than type. Letter-spacing, the speed of writing, and the letterer's character and emotions can all make a difference. And of course, they exude warmth.

Define good hand-lettering.

Good work transmits messages or projects a purpose.

How do you work from conception to execution?

I start with collecting what I need to know, before extracting what's needed to be drawn. Prior to deciding on a style and the nuances needed, I chew over the message to make sure I can deliver it accurately while making my work pleasant to the eyes. Using illustrations to draw attention and

letters to tell the necessary information gives the message greater depth. That way I also have more control over how the message is perceived.

How do you choose the mediums to work with and what do you use to create?

It depends on the location, the material I need to draw on and the purpose of the work. But my most-used tools are chalk, inerasable chalk marker and fountain pen. There are certain effects that only chalk and blackboard can achieve, such as slurs, blurs, textures, erasures. The chemistry between chalk and blackboard is unique.

Name one most common misconception about hand-lettering you know and tell us the truth.

You don't have to be a professional to draw beautiful letters.

tokyobike BLACK LIMITED, 2016.

Chalk on blackboard. Live signage-drawing at the promotion event for tokyobike's new bicycle frame. Commissioned by DENTSU INC. and tokyobike inc.

1

2

3

4

1-4/ Jazzy Sport, 2015.

Chalk and marker on blackboard, wood and glass. Window graphics and signage for a record store in Shimokitazawa, Tokyo and its pop-up shop at Paddlers Coffee Nishihara.

5-6/ Cafe&Bar 3rd, 2015.

Chalk on blackboard. Double-sided signage for a café and bar in Toyooka, Japan. Commissioned by DENTSU INC.

5, 6

7/ Golden Week Photo Booth, 2016.

Chalk on blackboard. Environmental graphics for a photo-taking event at department store LUMINE Ikebukuro during its golden week promotion. Commissioned by DENTSU INC. and H.P.FRANCE S.A.

8/ Coffee Lab, 2016.

Chalk on blackboard. Interior graphics for a pop-up shop of coffee bean chocolates. A collaboration between chocolatier Morozoff and ONIBUS coffee. Commissioned by DENTSU INC.

7

8

Daimaru Kyoto Dai Kujaku Sai, 2015.
Chalk and marker on blackboard. Window display for the Dai Kujaku festival promotion at Daimaru Matsuzakaya Department Stores Co. Ltd. Commissioned by DENTSU INC.

Portrait by Low Weakness

RYLSEE

Berlin, Germany
IG/FB:rylsee

Creating under the alias RYLSEE, Cyril Vouilloz loves to instil moments of mundane city life into hand-drawn letters. His own brand of graphic humour spices up murals, installations and items on SNEEER.com, a clothing label he started with his brother.

How did you become a letterer?

Letters and logos are something I've always been drawn to. When I was teenager, all I cared about was skateboarding, which along the way taught me about design, photography, graphic composition, film, music and friendship. But it is only during my studies in graphic design in Geneva, that I truly learnt about "proper typography" and that it is a bit too restrictive for me. I started to play with type and mix graffiti, illustration and a bit of everything I like in my work. It took me years of experimentation, so if you are feeling stuck in the grey zone, my advice is to follow what your guts tell you, and you'll find your way.

Do you see yourself more as a designer or a calligrapher?

Well, I'm just having fun with letters.

What's your creative style?

It's like a milkshake flavour where I blend together humour, lettering, graffiti, illustration and design.

What role does hand-lettering play in different areas of our visual world today?

I believe what's interesting about letters is that almost everybody can relate to the discipline because (almost) everybody writes. Letters give me the power to share ideas, thoughts and lame jokes with the world. I deeply like the idea that a drawing I post online or paint on a wall can potentially make someone's day! :)

Define good hand-lettering.

As I say in my Skillshare class, if you can hear the sound of your drawing it means you're on the right way.

How do you work from conception to execution?

I always have my sketchbook with me. Writing thoughts down, "stealing" from people's conversations in the metro or reading stuff on walls is part of my daily creative process. I then try to visually translate what surrounds me in the everyday life into some thoughtful font compositions. Most of my font compositions, as complex as they appear, are all born from a simple idea. What seems to touch fans of my work most is the honesty in it. I said to a friend one day that "I would never trust someone who doesn't like pizza." We both laughed out loud at this statement, and I thought: This is a great life advice that I should share with the world!

How do you choose the mediums to work with and what do you use?

Even though a lot of my work is on paper, I feel comfortable using pretty much all kinds of mediums. I love to create regardless of the medium. I suppose the sketchbook is just the most convenient option. Hehehe. :)

Name one most common misconception about hand-lettering you know and tell us the truth.

Well done doesn't mean interesting.

Drying Time, 2014. Acrylic on plywood.

017

Guess What?, 2014.

Ink on paper. Latin alphabet for solo exhibitions in art spaces Zimmer in Tel-Aviv, Israel and Art By Friends in Annecy, France. Each letter was illustrated to embody a word and viewers are encouraged to guess them with each other's help.

1/ Randomness of the night, 2016. Spray paint on concrete. Improvised mural at Urban Spree in Berlin, Germany to illustrate the concept of organised chaos.

2/ DYSTORPIA, 2016. Acrylic on plywood. Installation at La Vallée Gallery in Brussels, Belgium and Urban Spree to experiment the deformations of a sheet of paper.

3/ **AAAAAA, 2014.** Spray paint on concrete. Mural for Art By Friends in Annecy, France. Photo by Pascal Gautherot.

4/ **Inglewood, 2015.** Acrylic on concrete. Interior graphics for Inglewood burger in Geneva, Switzerland.

Here's to the ones who dream foolish, as they may seem Here's to the hearts that ache Here's to the mess we make

Homage to La La Land, 2016.
Pointed pen on watercolour paper. Freehand modern script with ink splatter design of an excerpt from *The Fools Who Dream*, a song from the movie *La La Land* (2016).

ANGI PHILLIPS

Brea, USA
IG/FB:angeliqueink

Angi Phillips is a graphic designer working mainly with her own freehand script calligraphy. She started her creative studio Angelique, Ink and takes on branding, product design and live hand-lettering projects. Angi also holds workshops to share her passion for pen and ink in the SoCal area, and occasionally other locations in the U.S. and overseas.

We're Better For All That We Let In, 2015.

Ink on paper digitalised for tattoo placement. Freehand script lettering for personal project. Tattoo by Jon at Old World Tattoo. Photo by Daniel Freeman.

How did you become a letterer? Do you see yourself more as a designer or a calligrapher?

My experience with calligraphy began at 12 when I was given a dip pen set for Christmas. I fell in love with the drawing of letters right then, particularly loving how ink bleeds into paper and the interesting pens that people don't see every day. After college, I practised calligraphy as a creative outlet, later finding out there is quite a demand for it. I consider myself a calligrapher who focuses on designs that incorporate handwritten elements.

What's your creative style?

My style is free, emotional, and perhaps dark but hopeful. I like to bend the rules of typography and calligraphy to allow for emotions and engagement.

What role does hand-lettering play in different areas of our visual world today?

Hand-lettering has seen a huge revival in recent years. It contrasts the clean, modern, minimalistic design styles of today, and calligraphy in particular weaves in a touch of randomness and surprise. Hand-lettering and calligraphy gives human touch to a design, something type isn't able to accomplish. It builds a connection between the giver and receiver.

Define good hand-lettering.

Good hand-lettering is concise, and delivers a message within the message. There is meaning in the words themselves, and meaning in the way the letters are created. Everything about how letters are formed should be intentional even when the project calls for something carefree.

How do you work from conception to execution?

My first sketches are to test out what styles, letterforms and layout relate best to the intended message. I then interpret ideas with pointed pen and ink, which always give different results from the initial pencil sketch because of the freedom of movement in handwritten works. I repeat this over and over, borrowing from each draft the stylistic nuances that work and eventually finding just the right balance and design.

How do you choose the mediums to work with and what do you use?

I'm fairly habitual about my go-to materials and tools, so I love it when clients request something different! I often use gouache instead of ink when I work with surfaces like wood and metal as it tends to adhere better, and use lettering brushes for large-scale pieces.

Name one most common misconception about hand-lettering you know and tell us the truth.

A common misconception is that one must have good handwriting in order to be good at hand-lettering or calligraphy. They are not about simply writing in one's natural cursive, but are broken down into sets of strokes and shapes, achieved by repeated practice of specific techniques.

1

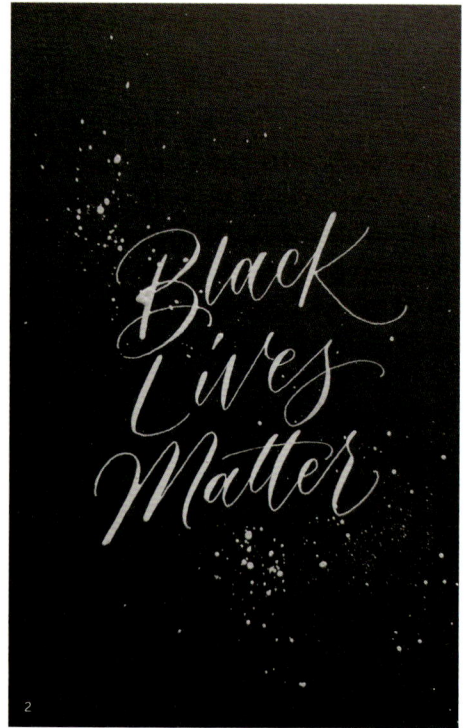

Black Lives Matter

2

3

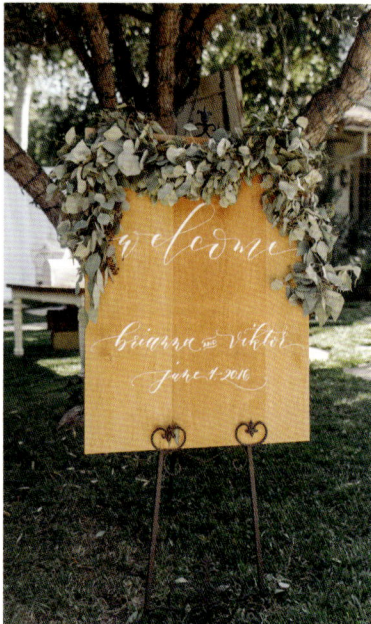

welcome

brianna and viktor

june 1, 2016

4

Only those who risk
going too far
can possibly find out
how far
one can go.

· TS ELIOT ·

5

1/ **Personal work, 2017.** Wood cut inkwell holders designed in-house, backdrop with pointed pen.

2/ **Black Lives Matter, 2020.** Bleed proof white ink on heavy black stock, hurried script for urgency effect. Photos zoom in closer with each crop for impact.

3/ **Brianna & Viktor, 2016.** Enamel on wood. Hand-painted welcome signage for Brianna Frolov's wedding. Photo by MK Sadler Photography. Wood board by Vintage Owl Rentals.

4/ **Risk, 2017.** Pointed pen with sumi ink on watercolor paper for social media.

5/ **Darkness & Light, 2016.** Enamel on concrete. Indoor mural commissioned by Laura Bishop, MD.

1 (opposite page), 2/ Mission Statement Panel Art, 2018. Large scale lettering design for FLDWRK with custom abstract script for 3-panel triptych artwork containing the company's mission statement. Plywood panels and latex paint. Wedding Photo by Sincerely Sini.

3/ Jorg & Morgan's Modern Sleek Acrylic Suite, 2019. Free script and modern elements, digitisation for foil press printing on acrylic pieces. Printing by Czar Press.

4/ Place Cards, 2019. Round place cards for event. Names scripted in white ink with pointed pen. Freehand modern script, engaging the edges of the card.

sans serifs no letters and no words to read sans words no signs no names in the streets just rows of buildings and gardens sans weeds

NIELS SHOE MEULMAN

Amsterdam, the Netherlands
IG/FB:nielsshoemeulman

Already a street art legend in the 1980s, Niels Shoe Meulman further his experiments on letterforms by starting Calligraffiti. Fusing bold attitude of his street days with the art of writing, the movement blazed a new trail in modern lettering. The visual artist's body of work and his creation of a unique style called 'Abstract Vandalism' is illustrated in his new book *Shoe is My Middle Name.*

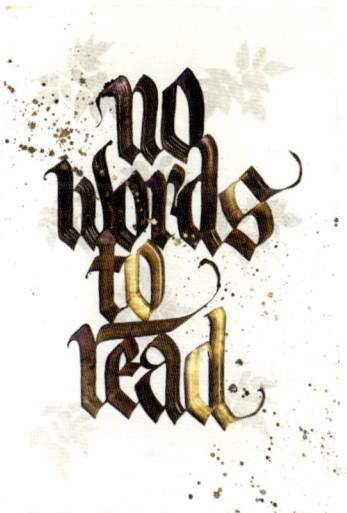

How did you become a letterer? Do you see yourself more as a designer or a calligrapher?

I transitioned from graffiti into typography design. I'm not really a designer nor a calligrapher but an abstract artist. Calligraphy to me is like a bridge that connects letters to abstract paintings.

What's your creative style?

I would consider my work "gestural paintings". They are abstract yet direct. If the ink goes on the paper, then that's it, you can't really change it anymore. All in all I try to keep a balance between my metropolitan attitude and a more natural style.

What role does hand-lettering play in different areas of our visual world today?

Hand-lettering was a common and ordinary practice three to four decades ago but with all the counter movements and digitalisation, it has become something special that people would appreciate more. On the other hand, technology has allowed us to share our work with the world. There's no good or bad about what it presents in the current culture. It's good as long as the art is not dying.

Define good hand-lettering.

One word: consistency. Even if the work looks strange or weird at first, it works if you keep it consistent.

How do you work from conception to execution?

Execution won't take long but conception is always ongoing, even at sleep. I stop thinking when I paint because it's hard to do two things at the same time which is the likely cause of spelling errors.

How do you choose the mediums to work with and what do you use?

A couple of years ago I realised that I could really write and paint with anything in hand. I once did some work on paper with a twig and mud. And my workshop has got brooms, brushes and sticks of all kind. When I was in India, brooms (those for sweeping) are seen everywhere. So I just pick one up and paint. I also like to use those made of long grass. I only use a little bit of colour here and there, with a lot of regular black ink and acrylic paint. Sometimes I use a bit of pearlescent and iridescent colours for painting as well.

Name one most common misconception about hand-lettering you know and tell us the truth.

People often think typography, calligraphy and lettering are the same thing but they aren't. Where type are produced by printing, hand-lettering is actually a type of drawing, like a sign; calligraphy is the art of writing.

1/Graffiti are the weeds of art, 2016. Various paint and plant brooms on concrete. Mural at New Delhi, India for St+Art India. Photo by Akshat Nauriyal.

2/No words to read, 2016. Acrylic and ink on handmade paper.

2

3-5

6, 7

3-5/ From Delhi to Nice I-III, 2016. Acrylic and ink on handmade paper.

6/ Even Eleven, 2014. Acrylic on linen.

7/ Alphabet Opus, 2014. Acrylic on canvas.

8/ Shoe's Shoes, 2015. An installation of sneakers worn by Niels Shoe Meulman between 1982 and 2014. Part of the Abstract Vandalism exhibition at Galerie Gabriel Rolt, Amsterdam, The Netherlands. Photo by Peter Tijhuis.

9

10, 11

12

10-11/ Mechanical S I-II, 2014.
Ink on mulberry paper.

12/ Missing words, 2015.
Ink on mulberry paper.

Abandoned House, 2016.

Acrylic on concrete. Mural painting at an
abandoned house in Sicily, Italy. Project by Blaqk.
Photo by Dimitris Vasiliou.

GREG PAPAGRIG-ORIOU @ BLAQK

Athens, Greece
URL:gregpapagrigoriou.tumblr.com

Keen on experimenting calligraphy with form, shapes, and lines, Greg Papagrigoriou teams up with designer-artist Chris Tzaferos, a.k.a. Simek, to form Blaqk. The duo manifests their unique take on letters, incorporating geometric compositions, textures and negative space into murals, paintings and graphic design.

How did you become a letterer? Do you see yourself more as a designer or a calligrapher?

I made first contact with typography and lettering during my graphic design training. I attended a calligraphy seminar near the end of my studies and was immediately captivated by the process. This was eight years ago when I started to rely more on my hands to create and experiment on different surfaces such as wall and paper. I see myself as a graphic designer/artist who create with calligraphy and letterforms.

What's your creative style?

You could say it is abstract calligraphy, that embraces geometric motifs common in Eastern and folk art.

What role does hand-lettering play in different areas of our visual world today?

It plays a very important role. It is the medium that conveys messages or information, and imparts the character and identity of this information in much the same way as how the sign of an ice-cream shop differs from the logo of a metal band. By using the same methods and materials as people hand-lettered before the digital era, it also connects the present and the past.

Define good hand-lettering.

Good hand-lettering rests on the principles of good calligraphy and typography. Although intrinsically different, they share some common rules on spacing, consistency and so on. A good understanding of all three disciplines will help one gain a comprehensive picture of how to create letters.

How do you work from conception to execution?

Once I know what my topic is, I will start figuring a way to visualise my ideas. I will conduct research and draft before deciding on an appropriate approach.

How do you choose the mediums to work with and what do you use?

It varies with projects. For logos, I use different brushes, pens or pencils. But if the work is done on walls or buildings, I usually make my own flat brush by connecting smaller brushes together.

Name one most common misconception about hand-lettering you know and tell us the truth.

Hand-lettering is often mistaken as equivalent to calligraphy. While the former is drawing, the latter is about writing beautiful letters with one stroke.

Zentai Teki Ni, The EP, 2014.

Album artwork for Greek DJ Billa Qause. Project by Greg Papagrigoriou. Printing by Symbolink. Photo by Antonis Katrakazis.

Blaqk Seikon, 2015.

Acrylic on concrete. Mural painting in Athens, Greece. A collaboration between Blaqk and Polish artist Seikon. Photo by Alka Murat.

Black Blaqk Lines, 2015.
Acrylic on wall. Mural painting at an apartment in Athens, Greece. Project by Blaqk. Photo by Dimitris Vasiliou.

Emergence Festival, 2015.

Acrylic on wall. Mural painting in Sicily, Italy. Project by Blaqk. Photo by Dimitris Vasiliou.

KATOL @ START FROM ZERO

Hong Kong
IG: ratscave_sfz
URL: katolone.tumblr.com

Hong Kong-born artist Katol Lo channels his creative energy and affinity for life through art shows, Dirty Boogie Rockabilly Festivals and art books (under the alias Bore Paper). He currently co-runs local street art group Start From Zero, street wear brand New York Monk Academy and Union Grocery in Taiwan.

How did you become a letterer? Do you see yourself more as a designer or a calligrapher?

It was around the year 2014 when I had a year off and the chance to watch documentary *Sign Painters* and the work of my friend Man Luk, who's probably the first to paint western-style signs in Hong Kong. I'm a designer who straddles fashion, graphic design and furniture design. Sign painting is my most recent favourite creative medium which I hope I can spend more time exploring.

What's your creative style?

I love vintage workwear, therefore I am very attached to old-time typographic designs and alignment. While creating, I also intend to infuse the graphic elements of old Hong Kong shop signs into my work.

What role does hand-lettering play in different areas of our visual world today?

I imagine most of us have been quite fed up with the impassive type. In that sense, hand-lettering and hand-painted signs are perhaps the most authentic kind of folk art. Every country has its own typographic style.

Define good hand-lettering.

The letterer's techniques, enthusiasm about the art and his or her attitude towards hand-lettering all play a part in shaping the letters. It is also a reflection of the letterer's personality. Creating signs as a gift is likened to writing love letters to your loved ones.

How do you work from conception to execution?

I normally start with manual drafts before processing my design on the computer and refining the work by hand, the rather non-traditional way.

How do you choose the mediums to work with and what do you use?

I use 1-Shot Lettering Enamels from the States and Handover brushes from UK. But what matters more is the idea behind each piece of work.

Name one most common misconception about hand-lettering you know and tell us the truth.

Many think of hand-lettering as colouring letters. In fact, it takes time and effort, repeated practice and an observant eye for everyday type work to perfect one's art. There's always a close connection between a letterer's tools and the strokes he or she designs. Whatever the subject, there's a wisdom to success.

1/ S.F.Z x WOAW Duck Defect Pop-up Store, 2016. Enamel on glass. Window graphics and signage for a pop-up shop of lifestyle goods co-designed by Start From Zero and concept store WOAW.

2/ Dust House, 2016. Gold leaf and enamel on glass. Window graphics for District Distribution Company Limited.

Wow & Flutter, 2016. Gold leaf and enamel on glass and wood. Installations for a Hong Kong music festival organised by 89268.

3/ SFZ, 2015. Enamel on glass and wood. Sign boards as interior graphics for Start From Zero.

4/ White Whale, 2016. Enamel on wood. Signage for a vintage clothing and leather goods store.

3, 4

5/ Hidden Agenda, 2016. Enamel on wood. Sign board for an indie livehouse in Hong Kong.

5

Gunglok Union Grocery, 2016. Gold leaf and enamel on glass and wood. Window graphics, signage and wall installation for a café and event space in Taipei, Taiwan.

Interview

R by Copenhagen Signs

1
RETRO VINTAGE
P.046 - P.073

2
EXTRAVAGANT CLASSICS
P.074 - P.097

3
BRUSH PEN CALLIGRAPHY
P.098 - P.125

4
ILLUSTRATIVE LETTERING
P.126 - P.165

5
MIXED STYLE
P.166 - P.191

I am Wasted Again / The Phantom Trail / Seven Days a Week - Print Shoppe
Media : Pencil, Felt Pen, Digital

RETRO VINTAGE

EXTRAVAGANT CLASSICS

BRUSH PEN CALLIGRAPHY

ILLUSTRATIVE LETTERING

MIXED STYLE

The Holy Cross Brewing Society / Granite State Apparel / Adventure Company
Media : Pencil, Felt Pen, Digital

TO
CREATE
WE MUST
DESTROY
STOFF AUS FRANKFURT

Stoff aus Frankfurt
Media : Pencil, Felt Pen, Digital

We Never Sleep / Never Get Enough / Cabinet of Curiosities / Back to the Roots

Media : Pencil, Felt Pen, Digital

VOID

Flourished V, X, Y, Z
Media : Pencil, Pigma Micron Pen, White Ink

RETRO VINTAGE

EXTRAVAGANT CLASSICS

BRUSH PEN CALLIGRAPHY

ILLUSTRATIVE LETTERING

MIXED STYLE

A
BCDE
FGHIJK
LMNOP
QRSTUV
WXYZ

Alphabet
Media : Rotring Pen, Arches Satin Paper

Hall & Marciniak
Media : Pencil

Swindler & Swindler

RETRO VINTAGE

EXTRAVAGANT CLASSICS

BRUSH PEN CALLIGRAPHY

ILLUSTRATIVE LETTERING

MIXED STYLE

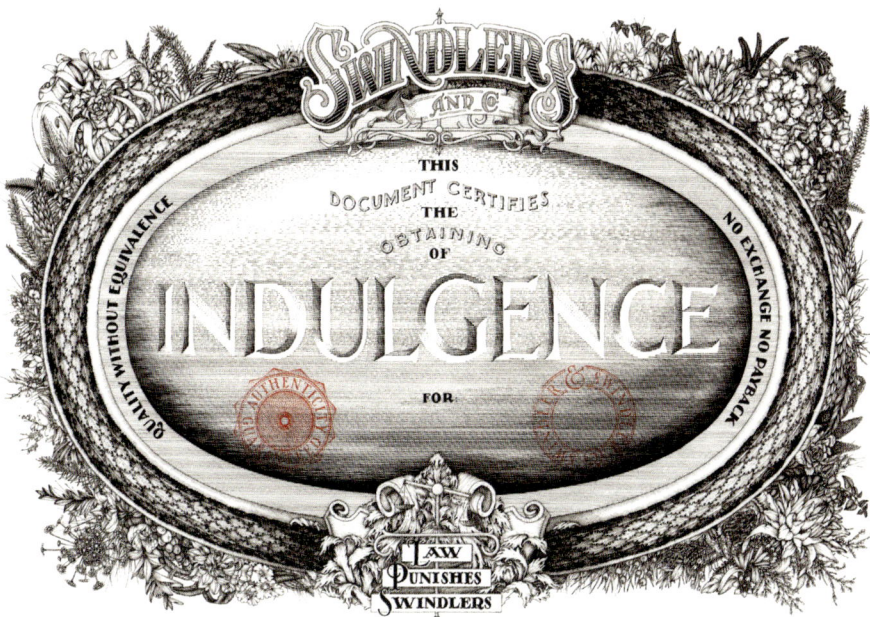

Honesty / Indulgence
Media : Rotring Pen, Arches Satin Paper

SWINDLERS

AND C.

THIS

DOCUMENT CERTIFIES

THE

OBTAINING

OF

AUTHENTICITY GUARANTEED

Self-Res

FOR

QUALITY WITHOUT EQUIVALENCE

Self-respect | Media : Rotring Pen, Arches Satin Paper

A GENTLEMAN IS SIMPLY A PATIENT WOLF

◆ LANA TURNER ◆

A Gentleman Is Simply A Patient Wolf
Media : 0.7mm Mechanical Pencil, Digital

THE OFFICIAL 2015 SXSWi CLOSING PARTY
PRESENTED BY MEDIA TEMPLE
TV On The
RADIO
with LUDACRIS
AND Z★TRIP

TUESDAY MARCH 17 8:30 TO 1:30
AT STUBB'S BBQ

OPEN TO PLATINUM, GOLD & INTERACTIVE PASSES
MEDIATEMPLE.NET/SXSW | @MEDIATEMPLE | #MTSXSW

(mt)
mediatemple

TV On The Radio SXSW Poster Lightning for Media Temple
Media : Pencil, Tracing Paper

The Bastard Executioner
Media : Pencil, Copic Wide Marker, Pigma Micron Pen, Tracing Paper

Brush Lettering 101 for Poketo / Lettering 101 for Summer Camp
Media : Pencil, Tracing Paper

No Fucking Instagrams for RVCC
Media : Pencil, Broad Nibbed Pen, Tracing Paper

Carmel Type Co
Media : Pencil, Digital, Tracing Paper

Drew Melton

RETRO VINTAGE

EXTRAVAGANT CLASSICS

BRUSH PEN CALLIGRAPHY

ILLUSTRATIVE LETTERING

MIXED STYLE

PARIS+FRANCE
♠
EPICURIAL
MOTORCYCLE
CLUB

PARIS
CUSTOM
7 EPICURIAL 5
MOTORCYCLE
CLUB

Epicurial
MED EMD

EPICURIAL™
EMD

Epicurial Motorcycle Club
Media : Pencil, Tracing Paper

Defend Paris / Say What Studio
Media : Pencil

McDonald's
Media : Pencil, Tracing Paper | Special credits : Costume 3 pièces, Tbwa Paris

HE PERFORMS
WONDERS
THAT CANNOT
BE FATHOMED
MIRACLES
THAT CANNOT
BE COUNTED

Daily Quotes
Media : Pencil

WHATEVER YOU DO
WORK
WITH ALL YOUR HEART

I SET YOU
WHEREVER
YOU ARE

Daily Quotes
Media : Pencil

Daily Quotes, 30 Days of Bible Lettering
Media : Pencil

Arrow Shirts for Phillips Van Husen, Arrow Shirt Co.
Media : Pencil, Brush, Watercolour Paint, Digital

Arrow Shirts for Phillips Van Husen, Arrow Shirt Co. | Media : Pencil, Brush, Watercolour Paint, Digital

Hello!

HELLO!

Spring

Hello!

Hello!

Connection

Struggle

Woodspiration Camp

HELLO!

Bonjour!

Hi Hi!

Ciao!

Random Tags and Logotypes
Media : Pencil, Pointed Brush, Line Pen, "Crown Multi" Permanent Marker, Ink, Tracing Paper

One More Bottle Beer Store
Media : 2H Pencil, Technical Drawing Pen, Sharpie Fine Marker, Tracing Paper

Black&White
Media : 2H Pencil, Technical Drawing Pen, Sharpie Fine Marker, Tracing Paper

FINALLY

Copenhagen

Finally / Copenhagen
Media : 0.5mm Staedtler Pigment Liner, Sharpie Fine Point Permanent Marker

NEVERTHELESS

Nevertheless
Media : 1-Shot Enamel Paint, Handover Sable Chisel Writer 2112 #12, Glass

Horror
Media : Automatic Pen

Nonetheless, Dr. Strange Love
Media : 0.5mm Staedtler Pigment Liner, Sharpie Fine Point Permanent Marker

Copenhagen Signs

RETRO VINTAGE

EXTRAVAGANT CLASSICS

BRUSH PEN CALLIGRAPHY

ILLUSTRATIVE LETTERING

MIXED STYLE

123
Media : Round Nib Calligraphy Pen

Experimental Round Nib Alphabet
Media : Round Nib Calligraphy Pen

Ged Palmer
Media : 1-Shot Enamel Paint, Dibond Panel

Under the Volcano. Bajo el vocán — Love of Lesbian for Nysu Films
Media : Tombow Marker, Digital

Bolt Motor Co.
Media : Graphite Pencil, Edding 1200, Digital

Hawkers & Wolfnoir for The Hawkers Co.
Media : Pocket Brush Pen, Fineliner

Grind
Media : Copic Multiliners

Expand
Media : White Marker, Copic Multiliners, Black Paper

Adrian Iorga

RETRO VINTAGE

EXTRAVAGANT CLASSICS

BRUSH PEN CALLIGRAPHY

ILLUSTRATIVE LETTERING

MIXED STYLE

Greetings from Dubaï

Thomas Savary

Sarah Vaughan

Greetings from Dubaï for Thomas Savary
Media : Pencil

BILL CUNNINGHAM

Freedom is the most expensive thing.

Daily Quotes
Media : Digital

LEARN
TO SPEAK WITH BOTH YOUR
Heart
and *Mind*
for
THE GROUND BENEATH
Will
Hold
you
DEAR

Know That
YOU'RE ...
Free

For My Daughter by Sarah McMane
Media : Mechanical Pencil, Digital

Daily Quotes, 30 days of Bible Lettering
Media : Pencil

A Moment of Thanks
Media : Brush, Pointed Pen

Love
Media : Brush, Faber-Castell's PITT Artist Pen, Sakura's Gelly-Roll Pen in White

Starfish and Coffee
Maple syrup and jam
Butterscotch clouds, a tangerine
And a side order of ham
If you set your mind free, baby
Maybe you'd understand
Starfish and Coffee
Maple syrup and jam

Starfish and Coffee for Vic Lee
Media : Pointed Pen

No matter where I find myself. May I always turn towards the things that nourish me

~ April Green ~

Quote by April Green
Media : Walnut ink, Pointed pen, Nib, Pastel paper

There is magic in the ordinary, there is beauty in the plain. Just look and soon you'll see nothing is ever the same.

~ m.b. victoria ~

Quote by M.B. Victoria
Media : Needle, Walnut ink, Pointed pen, Nib, Pastel paper

Quote by Gemma Troy
Media : Metallic watercolour, Pointed pen, Nib, Sketch book paper

Quote by Gemma Troy
Media : Metallic watercolour, Pointed pen, Nib, Watercolor paper

RETRO VINTAGE

EXTRAVAGANT CLASSICS

BRUSH PEN CALLIGRAPHY

ILLUSTRATIVE LETTERING

MIXED STYLE

No matter what
life may present
I will always be
capable, content
and complete

~ Harpreet M Dayal ~

Quote by Harpreet M Dayal
Media : Dr. Martin's Bleed Proof White Ink, Pointed pen, Nib, Pastel paper

Love yourself

with such abundance

that it flows to those

around you

— a elle poetry —

Quote by ELLE Poetry
Media : Dr. Martin's Bleed Proof White Ink, Pointed pen, Nib, Pastel paper

A Moment of Thanks
Media : Pointed Pen

Pencil Letters
Media : Mechanical Pencil, Pigma Micron Pen, Tracing Paper | Special credits : Jake Weidmann

1 in 88 for Sevenly
Media : Pencil, Pigma Micron Pen, Tracing Paper

Uncork The Night
Media : 2B Lead Staedtler Mechanical Pencil,
Tracing Paper, Digital

Every Person Matters
Media : Mechanical Pencil, Tracing Paper

2010

HANDSOME
Devil

CALIFORNIA RED

Cabernet Sauvignon

Handsome Devil Sketch
Media : Pencil, Digital

Stoff aus Frankfurt
Media : Pencil, Felt Pen, Digital

RETRO VINTAGE

EXTRAVAGANT CLASSICS

BRUSH PEN CALLIGRAPHY

ILLUSTRATIVE LETTERING

MIXED STYLE

Black Sheep / Thirsty / Villar Rodriguez
Media : Pencil, Digital

THE

Hart & Iron

SUPPLY Co

SACRAMENTO CA.

Hart & Iron Supply Co.
Media : Graphite Pencil, Dual Brush Marker, Digital

Drinksmith

The Essentials

Drinksmith / The Essentials for SDH
Media : Graphite Pencil, Fineliner, Digital

Logo for ETLettering
Media : Point Nib Pen

Cult de Moir
Media : Pencil, Digital

Logo for Etudesite.ru Workshop in Moscow
Media : Pencil, Broad Nib Pen

Thank You Cards
Media : Brause 361 Steno Blue Pumpkin Nib, Moon Palace Sumi Ink

It Was Always You
Media : Brause 66EF Nib, Moon Palace Sumi ink

Merry Christmas

Joy to the World

Christmas Cards
Media : Brause 66EF Nib, Moon Palace Sumi Ink

Calligraphy is my Therapy

Therapy
Media : Walnut Ink or Calligraphy Gouache,
Oblique holder, EF Principal

D.LEONARDT & Co
TRADE
MARK
BIRMINGHAM.

Empathy
Media : Walnut Ink or Calligraphy Gouache, Oblique holder,
EF Principal & Nikko G nibs

Friend
Media : Walnut Ink or Calligraphy Gouache, Oblique holder,
EF Principal & Nikko G nibs

Keep Calm
&
Practice
Calligraphy
and social distancing

Keep Calm
Media : Walnut Ink or Calligraphy Gouache, Oblique holder,
EF Principal & Nikko G nibs

Practice
Makes
Progress

Progress Big
Media : Walnut Ink or Calligraphy Gouache, Oblique holder,
EF Principal & Nikko G nibs

RETRO VINTAGE

EXTRAVAGANT CLASSICS

BRUSH PEN CALLIGRAPHY

ILLUSTRATIVE LETTERING

MIXED STYLE

Perfection is achieved not when there is nothing more to add but when there is nothing left to take away

Perfection
Media : Walnut Ink or Calligraphy Gouache, Oblique holder,
EF Principal & Nikko G nibs

Be with someone who
fights for you,
someone who knows
you are worth it,
someone who knows
love is worth it.

— j.ironword —

Poem by J Iron Word for Lettering Challenge by @calligraphiewithliz
Media : Dr. Ph. Martin's iridescent ink 6R Jade, 15R Bronze, oblique pen holder, Hunt 101 nib

I hope you don't give up
when your sky fail to shine
for the sun may take a little longer
but the morning is on its way.

— Sonia —

Poem by Sonia for Lettering Challenge by @calligraphiewithliz
Media : Sennelier ink 405 Red Brown, oblique pen holder, Hunt 101 nib

If bad yesterday doesn't mean
a bad today,
The person you used to be,
doesn't define
who you can become.

— f.e.marie —

Poem by F. E. Marie for Lettering Challenge by @calligraphiewithliz
Media : Sumi ink, oblique pen holder, Hunt 101 nib

You Never Know How Strong You Are

until being strong is

the only choice

you have

— BOB MARLEY —

You Never Know How Strong You Are - Bob Marley
Media : Sumi ink, Oblique pen holder, Hunt 101 nib

Lose Your Inhibitions
Media : Sumi ink, Oblique pen holder, G-nib

And in that
moment I
swear we
were
infinite.

Even the
darkest
night will
end and
the sun
will rise

We Were Infinite / The Darkest Night
Media : Pointed Pen, Brush Pen, Water Brush, Watercolour, Liquid Water Colour, Watercolour Paper

"Why did you do all this for me?" HE ASKED.

"I don't deserve it. I've never done anything for you."

"You have been my friend," REPLIED CHARLOTTE.

"That in itself is a tremendous thing."

Charlotte's Web
Media : Pointed Pen, Brush Pen, Water Brush, Watercolour, Liquid Water Colour, Watercolour Paper

ROWENA RAVENCLAW

@ronnycakes

Wit Beyond Measure
Media : Pointed Pen, Brush Pen, Water Brush, Watercolour, Liquid Water Colour, Watercolour Paper

LES BROWN

C. S. LEWIS

-SOCRATES-

Sharon Tan

RETRO VINTAGE

EXTRAVAGANT CLASSICS

BRUSH PEN CALLIGRAPHY

ILLUSTRATIVE LETTERING

MIXED STYLE

Shoot For The Moon / Dream Another Dream / Be Slow To Fall Into Friendship / Your Quote Here
Media : Pointed Pen, Brush Pen, Water Brush, Watercolour, Liquid Water Colour, Watercolour Paper

Shopify Mural | Media : Brush, Acrylic

Inauthentic
Media : Pigma Micron Pen, Gold Ink, Black Paper

I Woke Up Like This
Media : Silver Ink, Metallic Gold Pigment, Letterpress

Nim Ben-Reuven

Flourished A / NOTHING MATTERS
Media : Pigma Micron Pen, Gold Ink, Black Paper

Beautiful

Beautiful for Manuscript
Media : Finetec Rose Gold Ink, TAKI-crafts holder, Manuscript Leonardt 300 Ballpoint Nib

Alphabet

Alphabet
Media : Kuretake ZIG Calligraphy metallic colours

Happy New Year

Happy New Year for Manuscript
Media : Finetec Arabic Gold Ink, TAKI-crafts holder, Manuscript Leonardt 33 nib

Autumn in the Air for Tombow
Media : Tombow Fudenosuke Hard Tip

Happy White Day
Media : Tombow Fudenosuke Hard Tip

RETRO VINTAGE

EXTRAVAGANT CLASSICS

BRUSH PEN CALLIGRAPHY

ILLUSTRATIVE LETTERING

MIXED STYLE

Fantastic for Manuscript
Media : Manuscript Callicreative Aquabrush Markers

Cosmos for Tombow
Media : Tombow ABT

Blessed
Media : Tombow ABT

Curiousity
Media : Zebra Fude-sign Midium Tip

Stay Safe
Media : Tombow ABT

flavours

sugar

BLACK PEPPER

dough nuts!

PEANUT BUTTER.

Brush Rush
Media : Brush Pen, Bush, Ink, Oil Pastel, Digital

Brush Rush
Media : Brush Pen, Bush, Ink, Oil Pastel, Digital

The National Christian Choir
Media : Brush Pen

Black Is My Happy Colour for State Bicycle Co.
Media : Crayola Marker

State Bicycle Co.
Media : Digital

The Draw Of Lettering for Stevenson University
Media : Pen, Paper, Digital

SuperWoman! for Crayligraphy
Media : Crayola Marker

RETRO VINTAGE

EXTRAVAGANT CLASSICS

BRUSH PEN CALLIGRAPHY

ILLUSTRATIVE LETTERING

MIXED STYLE

Smokestack Lightning
Media : Copic Multiliners

Silence
Media : White Pen, Black Construction Paper

Adrian Iorga

120
|
121

No Monday Blues Here!
Media : Crayola Pip Squeaks, Brush

Fly Me To The Moon!
Media : Tombow Dual Brush Marker, Brush

Be Productive / Be So Good...
Media : Tombow Dual Brush Marker, Brush

EXPLOSIONS
IN THE SKY

RIDE
THE
WAVE

HERE'S
TO THE
CRAZY
ONES

Brush Rush
Media : Brush Pen, Bush, Ink, Oil Pastel, Digital

Russian Yoga Festival / ZooYork T-shirt
Media : Oriental Brush

Paleta Handmade Ice-cream
Media : Ruling Pen

G-Easy T-shirt
Media : Pointed Brush

WORK SHOP

TOKYO / APRIL 16

BE THE THING THAT STARTS THE STUFF

Workshop in Tokyo / Umano Clothing
Media : Customised Pentel Brush Pen, Black Ink

Do What You Do Best
Media : Homemade Pen Made From Cola Can, Black Ink

RETRO VINTAGE

EXTRAVAGANT CLASSICS

BRUSH PEN CALLIGRAPHY

ILLUSTRATIVE LETTERING

MIXED STYLE

Personal Letter - B
Media : Wide Rough Brush, Black Ink

Personal Letter - B
Media : Homemade Pen Made From
350g Business Card, Black Ink

Personal Letter - R, Z
Media : Wide Foam Brush, White Sumi Ink

Silly
Media : Ruling Pen, White Sumi Ink

Travel
Media : Folded Ruling Pen, Black Ink

Promotion for Tokyo Workshop
Media : Homemade Pen Made From Cola Can, White Sumi Ink

Au Revoir
Media : Ruling Pen, Black Ink

RETRO VINTAGE

EXTRAVAGANT CLASSICS

BRUSH PEN CALLIGRAPHY

ILLUSTRATIVE LETTERING

MIXED STYLE

Skate Or Die / Love Your Life
Media : Brush, Ink

Lookbook
Media : Homemade Brush Pen

Dope Cans
Media : Brush, Ink

Zolifornia Love
Media : Homemade Brush Pen

GOOD LOOKING
STUDIO

It's Handpainted
Media : Kuretake Brush Pen

Hard 2 Buff
Media : Homemade Ruling Pen

JustWannaParty
Crew®

Out for Fame 2
Media : Homemade Ruling Pen

Yes You Can
Media : Brush, Ink

Alphabet
Media : Kuretake Brush Pen

The Quick Foxy Brown - Snoop Dogg
Media : Kuretake Brush Pen

From Line to Letters, From Letters to Everywhere
Media : Brush Pen, Ink

From Line to Letters, From Letters to Everywhere
Media : Brush Pen, Ink

From Line to Letters, From Letters to Everywhere
Media : Brush Pen, Ink

RETRO VINTAGE

EXTRAVAGANT CLASSICS

BRUSH PEN CALLIGRAPHY

ILLUSTRATIVE LETTERING

MIXED STYLE

Print for Antimony Clothing by Christopher Azevedo
Media : Pilot Parallel Pen, Watercolour, Textured Paper, Digital

Miracles Still Happen (With Or Without You)
Media : Pencil, Paper, Digital

Vlada Ruzhitskaya

RETRO VINTAGE

EXTRAVAGANT CLASSICS

BRUSH PEN CALLIGRAPHY

ILLUSTRATIVE LETTERING

MIXED STYLE

The Magic Is Not In The Things, But In The Approach Towards These Things
-Salvador Dali.
Media : Pencil, Paper, Digital

Vlada Ruzhitskaya

For Whom The Moon Shines, The Stars Also Smile
Media : Ink, Brush, Paper, Digital

Dripping Water Hollows Out Stone (Quote by Ovid) &
You Can Do Any Difficult Job Thanks To Patience (Russian Proverb)
Media : Ink, Brush, Paper, Digital

We Knit A Vyaz (Word Game)
Media : Pencil, Paper, Digital

Vlada Ruzhitskaya

RETRO VINTAGE

EXTRAVAGANT CLASSICS

BRUSH PEN CALLIGRAPHY

ILLUSTRATIVE LETTERING

MIXED STYLE

Day Of Slavic Writing And Culture. This Is A Russian Holiday, Celebrated On May 24.
Media : Ink, Brush, Paper, Digital

Vlada Ruzhitskaya

RETRO VINTAGE

EXTRAVAGANT CLASSICS

BRUSH PEN CALLIGRAPHY

ILLUSTRATIVE LETTERING

MIXED STYLE

Every House Has Its Own Special Rules
Media : Ink, Cola Pen, Paper, Digital

B&W Calligraphy / Tattoo For Ivo Abbiati
Media : Pilot Parallel Pen, Brush, Watercolour, Textured Paper, Digital

B&W Calligraphy
Media : Pilot Parallel Pen, Brush, Watercolour, Textured Paper, Digital

Only Human After All
Media : Brush, Acrylic, Digital

Blurring The Lines Between Earth And Mind
Media : Brush, Acrylic, Digital

RETRO VINTAGE

EXTRAVAGANT CLASSICS

BRUSH PEN CALLIGRAPHY

ILLUSTRATIVE LETTERING

MIXED STYLE

WE DO

We Do
Media : Brush, Ink, Digital

THE ONLY WAY IS UP

The Only Way Is Up
Media : Brush, Acrylic, Digital

HUSTLE HARD STAY HUMBLE

RIDE THE WAVES WITH ME

Hustle Hard Stay Humble / Ride The Waves With Me
Media : Brush, Acrylic, Digital

Pissed Modernism for Want Some Studio
Media : Dry-erase Marker, Dry-erase White Board, Small Eraser, Finger, Digital

Work Until Idols Become Rivals
Media : Dry-erase Marker, Dry-erase White Board, Small Eraser, Finger, Digital

Say What Studio Original
Media : Pen, Watercolour

Strength in Letters
Media : Pencil

Still Works Lettering
Media : Pencil

Pointless Ligatures EVERYWHERE!

CHEAP TRICK *Lettering* ADVICE № 1

Place YOUR MESSY TYPE Over A Nice PHOTO

CHEAP TRICK!

Cheap Trick
Media : Pencil, Digital

Please Send Queso for Ryan Carroll / Logo for Hunter Sprague Photography
Media : Pencil, Digital

Rickard's Movember for Rickard's
Media : Pencil, Digital | Creative direction : Alex Bakker

PLANS ARE ONLY GOOD INTENTIONS UNLESS THEY IMMEDIATELY DEGENERATE INTO HARD WORK

RETRO VINTAGE

EXTRAVAGANT CLASSICS

BRUSH PEN CALLIGRAPHY

ILLUSTRATIVE LETTERING

MIXED STYLE

Good Magazine Promotional Card
Media : Pencil, Digital | Art direction : Joseph Vandernorth | Copywriting : Peter Drucker

Inkonsky Logotype
Media : Pencil, Pigma Micron Pen 01, Digital

BLACK & WHITE
Media : Black Pen, Pencil

BLACK & WHITE
Media : Black Pen, Pencil

LOS YORK
Media : Manga Screentones, Black Pen

MAKE EVERYDAY EARTH DAY
Media : Black Pen, Digital

BLACK & WHITE
Media : Black Pen, Pencil

CARHARTT FW13
Media : Pencil

COLOSSAL for Colossal Media
Media : Colour Pencil, Pencil

ALL YOU NEED IS NATURE for Bonobo Jeans
Media : Colour Pencil, Pencil

Shout Out
Media : Pigma Micron Fineliner

Solid / Nirvana
Media : Pigma Micron Fineliner

For The Love of Letterforms / Whats Real Is What You Feel
Media : Pigma Micron Fineliner

What We Think / Work Hard Stand Proud / Homies Help Homies
Media : Copic Multiliners

TIME for a Change TIME TO Move On!
.MLYHR.

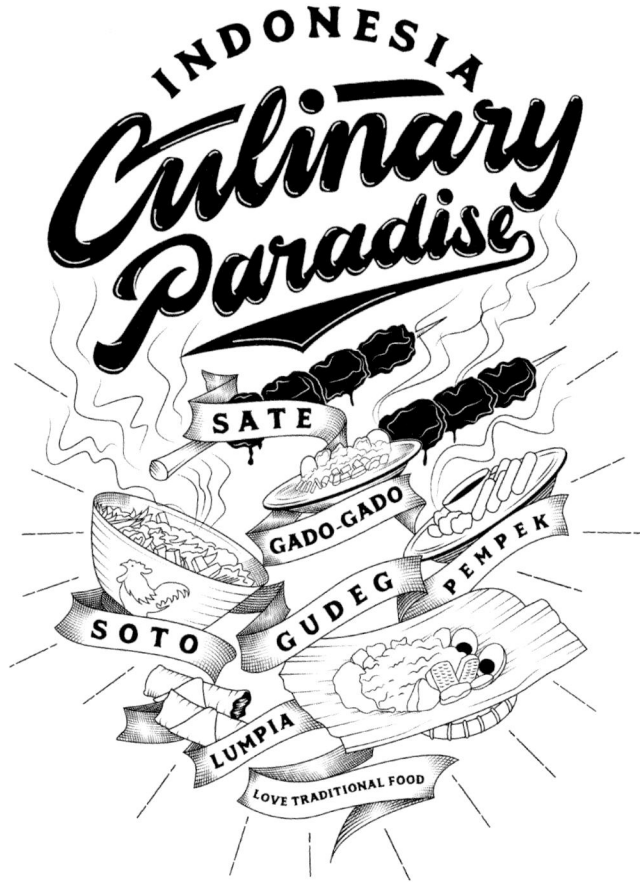

INDONESIA Culinary Paradise

SATE

GADO-GADO

SOTO   GUDEG   PEMPEK

LUMPIA

LOVE TRADITIONAL FOOD

Time For a Change
Media : Derwent Graphik Pen, Sakura Gelly Roll Pen

INDONESIA CULINARY PARADISE for FOODCLOTA
Media : Derwent Graphik Pen

Patience Ensures Victory / Top of The Morning for you
Media : Derwent Graphik Pen, Sakura Gelly Roll Pen

Traffic Jam Free
Media : Derwent Graphik Pen, Sakura Gelly Roll Pen

Time Flies, But You Are The Pilot
Media : Derwent Graphik Pen, Sakura Gelly Roll Pen

Take Me Down Into The Deep Dark Sea
Media : Sakura Gelly Roll Pen

HUSTLE & BUSTLE for NIKE
Media : Pencil, Sharpie Marker, Sakura Gelly Roll Pen

Wake Up, Kick Ass, Be Kind, Repeat
Media : Derwent Graphik Pen

With Sunrise We Rise
Media : Sakura Gelly Roll Pen

Riki harimulya

RETRO VINTAGE

EXTRAVAGANT CLASSICS

BRUSH PEN CALLIGRAPHY

ILLUSTRATIVE LETTERING

MIXED STYLE

Wish From A Bone

Smoke My Friends / Little Drop Of Poison
Media : 0.7mm Mechanical Pencil, Behance Dot Grid Book, Digital

Diana Ross for Hard Rock International
Media : Pencil, Brush, Watercolour, Digital

Hard Rock Headstock for Hard Rock International
Media : Pencil, Brush, Watercolour, Digital

Beatles Branding for Universal Music Group
Media : Pencil, Brush, Watercolour, Digital

Romeo and Juliet for Ruffian Company
Media : Pencil, Brush, Watercolour, Digital

Secret Society Cigars for Ivy Cigar Co.
Media : Pencil, Brush, Gauche, Digital

Motley Crue Motorcycle for Hard Rock International
Media : Pencil, Brush, Watercolour, Digital

Take the High Road for Vans
Media : Pencil, Digital

Nothing But Heartache
Media : Pencil, Digital

Come in We're OPEN

OPEN 24 HOURS

CA$H FOR GOLD

BUY SELL LOAN

GUNS BOUGHT & SOLD

Lamberti

Diamonds JEWELLERY stereos

CASH LOANS

PAWN FAST

Mingo Lamberti "Pawn Shop" T-shirt Range
Media : Pencil, Digital

THIS HERE BooK IS THE PORTFOLIO

BOOK OF

Justin Poulter

ILLUSTRATOR & LETTERER REPRESENTED BY

SNYDER N.Y.

Somewhere Over The Rainbow - Sketch
Media : Faber-Castell PITT Artist Pen

RETRO VINTAGE

EXTRAVAGANT CLASSICS

BRUSH PEN CALLIGRAPHY

ILLUSTRATIVE LETTERING

MIXED STYLE

Bone China on a Budget - Give a St**
Media : Ballpoint Pen, Disposable Paper Plate

Bone China on a Budget - Take time
Media : Ballpoint Pen, Disposable Paper Plate

Bone China on a Budget - Eat Me
Media : Ballpoint Pen, Disposable Paper Plate

Coffee Time Selection | Media : Pen, Pencil, Paint, Ink

Chalkboy
IS HEADING TO

NORITAKE no MORI

N A G O Y A

Sunday 4TH SEP.

CHALKBOY & ONIBUS COFFEE

Hand
DRIPPING

Hand
WRITTING

&

CHALKBOY

Workshop!

ON SATURDAY 24TH OCTOBER

Len
KYOTO KAWARAMACHI

CHALKBOY'S
COMING &
G!

*Live
Painting*

AT

10TH
OCT.

CBM

OFURO CAFE
UTATANE

CHALKBOY & SIS's

Bird

workshop

Live drawing

CBM

SIS

D A I K A N   Y A M A

ON SUNDAY 16TH OCTOBER

WORKSHOP graphics
Media : Fountain Pen, Marker, Ink

CHALKBOY

RETRO VINTAGE

EXTRAVAGANT CLASSICS

BRUSH PEN CALLIGRAPHY

ILLUSTRATIVE LETTERING

MIXED STYLE

KIRIN Hard cidre for DENTSU INC.
Media : Fountain Pen, Ink

KIRIN Hard cidre for DENTSU INC.
Media : Chalk

RETRO VINTAGE

EXTRAVAGANT CLASSICS

BRUSH PEN CALLIGRAPHY

ILLUSTRATIVE LETTERING

MIXED STYLE

The Chase Barbershop
Media : Chalkboard Paint Covered Wood Board, White Pencil,
Acrylic Paint Pens (Posca and Molotow), Clear Adhesive Spray

AND WE KNOW THAT GOD CAUSES ALL THINGS To Work TOGETHER FOR GOOD TO THOSE WHO LOVE GOD TO THOSE WHO ARE CALLED ACCORDING To His PURPOSE ROMANS 8:28

All Things For Good

Media : Copic SP Multiliner Pens, Tombow Dual Brush Pen,
Koh-I-Noor 5616 Lead Holder, Strathmore 400 Drawing Paper

Fearfully and Wonderfully Made / Better Than I Deserve / Turn Your Eyes Upon Jesus
Media : Copic SP Multiliner Pens, Tombow Dual Brush Pen,
Koh-I-Noor 5616 Lead Holder, Strathmore 400 Drawing Paper

Believe THERE IS A GREAT POWER Silently WORKING ALL THINGS FOR GOOD

Greater Good by Beatrix Potter
Media : Pencil

GOD DIDN'T bring YOU THIS FAR TO LEAVE YOU

Daily Quotes , 30 Days of Bible Lettering
Media : Pencil

For EVERYTHING There is A SEASON A TIME FOR EVERY Matter UNDER HEAVEN

Ecclesiastes 3:1
Media : Pencil

YOU Think THE
ONLY PEOPLE
WHO ARE
PEOPLE
ARE PEOPLE WHO
Look & Think
LIKE YOU
BUT IF YOU WALK THE
FOOTSTEPS
of
A STRANGER
YOU'LL LEARN THINGS
YOU Never Knew YOU
NEVER KNEW

Color of The Wind
Media : Mechanical Pencil

Novia Jonatan

RETRO VINTAGE

EXTRAVAGANT CLASSICS

BRUSH PEN CALLIGRAPHY

ILLUSTRATIVE LETTERING

MIXED STYLE

Sketch Drunk Vector Sober
Media : Rotring 800 Mechanical Pencil

Go Flex / That Part
Media : Copic Multiliners

Lemn Bun - Good Wood, Bad Wood, Same Ash, Different Flame / Whoa Whoa Whoa
Media : Copic Multiliners

Be the SPARK THAT ignites the FLAME

Mudita's Art Gallery
Media : Pencil, Digital | Special credits : SportForTheWorld

Erasmus Barcelona Experience
Media : Pencil, Digital

Fuck Off and Die!
Media : Pigma Micron Pen 05, Zebra Brush Pen
Special credits : BAM! creative studio

BE THE INSPIRATION THE THIEF IS LOOKING FOR

up ↑

← too thick

← smaller

thickness spacing

Be The Inspiration for Tits and Tats
Media : Pencil, Ecoline

Paper Towns
Media : Pencil, Brush, Watercolour

PACK lighter GO Further

GO AFTER what it is THAT CREATES Meaning — IN YOUR LIFE
THEN trust YOURSELF TO HANDLE THE STRESS THAT FOLLOWS
ABC   Kelly McGonigal

Choose TO only SEE the GOOD Stuff

Fate loves the Fearless
ABC

Pack Lighter, Go Further / Find Meaning / Good Stuff / Brave
Media : Pencil, Brush, Watercolour

EVERY JOURNEY STARTS WITH A FIRST STEP.

SHARE your HEART WITH YOUR art

To MAKE LIVING ITSELF AN ART THAT IS THE Goal
Henry Miller

QUIET MORNINGS & SILENT nights IN THE ATTIC

Journey / Share / Living / Quiet Nights
Media : Pencil, Brush, Watercolour

Hello Postcard
Media : Pencil, Pointed Brush, Ink, Tracing Paper

This of The Obvious and Do the Opposite for Print Club London
Media : Mack Water-based Brush, Handover 333 Synthetic Brush, Water-based paint, Acetate

Tales of a Traveling Sign Painter for Better Letters
Media : Mack Water-based Brush, Handover 333 Synthetic Brush, Water-based paint

Mike Meyer Hand-Lettering Workshop by Better Letters: London Design Festival and London Fields
Media : Mack Water-based Brush, Handover 333 Synthetic Brush, Water-based paint

Mike Meyer Hand-Lettering Workshop by Better Letters: Mazeppa /
Tales of a Traveling Sign Painter
Media : Mack Water-based Brush, Handover 333 Synthetic Brush, Water-based paint

I JUST WANT TO DRINK C... EATE STUFF SLEEP

RETRO VINTAGE

EXTRAVAGANT CLASSICS

BRUSH PEN CALLIGRAPHY

ILLUSTRATIVE LETTERING

MIXED STYLE

Project Spaces Mural | Media : Brush, Marker, Acrylic

The page has a vertical author name "Tristan Kerr" in the left margin, a large photograph of a mural, page numbers 214|215 at bottom left, and a caption at bottom.

Wonderwalls Festival Mural, Port Adelaide
Media : Spray Paint

Going Nowhere but Here
Media : Acrylic, Spray Paint | Photo: Tash McCammon

The DRAW OF Lettering

A GUIDE TO GETTING STARTED

Hand-lettering and calligraphy are age-old skills that have made a huge resurgence in the last several years. The former being the art of drawing letterforms, and the latter the art of writing beautifully. While each practice utilises definitive methods, both are able to evoke feelings or moods simply by applying stylistic attributes to letterforms.

People often wonder what tools are needed to begin practising the crafts. The answer is quite simple. If your instrument of choice emits some kind of ink, graphite, paint, or really anything at all, then you have what you need. Tools don't make the craftsman; the amount of purposeful practice does.

Although there is no one pen that could make you more successful, some do help you in your efforts when starting out. For calligraphy, I point beginners in the direction of a firmer tip before using brush. Broad tip markers (e.g. Crayola markers) are an excellent choice — the nib is harder than most brush pens to allow for more resistance between the pen and the paper, which makes writing much easier, while the subtle flex is enough for thinner upstrokes and broad edge for thicker downstrokes.

Letters are inherently made by writing, so the continual practice of calligraphy will make understanding letterforms easier than trying your hand at hand-lettering first. But there's no strict rule. Start one or the other, or go ahead and try both. If you are more comfortable with illustration, then hand-lettering is your best bet. All you need is a #2 pencil. If you enjoy penmanship over drawing, calligraphy is the way to go.

One practice leads to another. Calligraphy and hand-lettering produce the same results — visually interesting letterforms that conjure their readers' emotions.

THE ANATOMY OF TYPE

Typographic terms for hand-lettering beginners

It's important for you to know the correct terminology before delving into letterforms. While terminology can vary depending on the style of writing, the following descriptions are used primarily in typography, lettering and calligraphy:

Ascender	The stem that extends above the waistline
Baseline	The Invisible line on which the majority of letters rest
Bowl	The curved shape that encloses the round part of a letter
Cross Stroke	The horizontal stroke that crosses a lowercase 't' or 'f'
Counter	The fully or partially enclosed interior space of a letter
Descender	The part of a letter that extends below the baseline
Entrance Stroke	A hairline lead-in stroke with which the letter begins
Exit Stroke	The hairline stroke with which the letter ends
Flourish	A decorative element added to compliment the letterform and the letters surrounding it
Hairline	The thinnest stroke (often the connector or entrance stroke)found in the letterform

CROSSBAR/LIGATURE · FLOURISH · ASCENDER · SWASH

Anatomy

HAIRLINE · BOWL · COUNTER · DESCENDER

Ligature	A character formed from two or more joined letters
Majuscule	An uppercase letter
Minuscule	A lowercase letter
Overshoot	The degree to which a round letter extends beyond the x-height to appear the same size as a flat letter at the same point size
Shoulder	The curve projecting from a stem in the lowercase 'h', 'm' and 'n'
Stem	The primary, diagonal or upright stroke in a letter
Swash	An exaggerated ornate end added to the first/last letter of a word
Terminal	The ends of any straight, diagonal or curved one strokes
Waistline	The invisible line running across the top of lowercase letters, also called 'median' or 'midline'
X-Height	The height of the lowercase 'x' used as a guideline for the height of other lowercase letters' main body

Text and images by Tierney Studio

THE FUNDAMENTALS OF HAND-LETTERING
Basic Principles & Tips

When starting off, try not to be too concerned with the correct angle, width or height of your strokes. Determine what is most comfortable for you. As long as there is some continuity and your slopes are consistent (try to avoid backsloping or excessive forward sloping) you'll find your way. If you use Crayola markers, writing is meant to be fun and relaxing, so make sure you are in the right mindset.

I would first like to stress two very important methods when practicing your basic strokes:

- **Upstrokes are thin**
- **Downstrokes are thick**

Embed this in your head so that it becomes second nature. Repeat these words each time you move the marker upwards and then downwards. If you happen to be one of those people who think aloud, make sure you isolate yourself from any living creature. This includes your cats.

HOW TO APPLY THIN UPSTROKES

Think about it—anytime you go against gravity, you're fighting nature. Maintaining a consistent upward movement is difficult. Whether you are using a metallic nib or brush pen, you have to pay close attention to your wrist and finger motion so that the point of the pen is able to glide across the paper without "catching." Of course, this is much easier said than done, but fear not! Try a marker to make your life a little easier when performing this task!

For thin upstrokes, use the tip of the marker with little finger pressure. This might sound crazy, but grip the barrel as if you are picking up a baby bird with your thumb, middle and index finger. I know you're an experienced hatchling caregiver, so imagining this shouldn't be too difficult.

While moving upwards, keep the marker as perpendicular to the paper as possible by bending your fingers and pulling them in towards the palm of your hand. This takes the broad edge out of play and allows for an easier coast as you are marking the paper.

Apply thin upstrokes by using the tip of the marker and the broad edge of the marker to apply thick downstrokes

The marker is almost perpendicular to the paper for thin upstrokes

minimum

HOW TO APPLY THICK DOWNSTROKES

Downstrokes can be a breath of fresh air after a session of hairline practice. As a matter of fact, I often find myself breathing in tandem with the movement of my marker. Try it out yourself—breathe in on the upstrokes, and exhale on the release of the downstroke. A great word to practice this technique is 'minimum.' When handling thick strokes, apply pressure and pull down, utilising the broad edge of the marker.

Contrary to keeping your marker perpendicular when managing your thin strokes, the angle at which the broad edge of the marker is able to rest horizontally in its most natural position, is best when applying your downstroke. By default, the edge of the marker will be able to do the job for you, but you shouldn't stop there.

The weight of your stroke is determined by the amount of pressure that is applied from your fingers, through the marker and onto the paper. You can vary your widths by shifting the tension within your fingertips. The firmer your grip on the barrel, the greater the force the marker has when pressed against the surface of the paper—creating broader stroke widths.

Depending how fast you move downwards, you'll be able to create different visual effects. Keep in mind, the faster your downstroke, the thinner the width. This quick movement permits smoother lines while also creating some really nice textures if you're going for that effect.

If you want thicker lines, move slowly. Pause on the initial mark, pull downwards and pause again to complete the stroke. You might find your lines seesaw when moving at this speed, but you'll discover through repeating this motion over and over again, that the shakiness isn't nearly as noticeable. Give it a go for ten more minutes and you'll remedy the problem naturally.

Remember, practice what feels most comfortable to you.

Don't be afraid to break below the baseline or above the waistline. Not every stroke needs to begin and end on the same line

Resting broad edge is best for thick downstrokes

Quick downstrokes create texture while slow downstrokes make broader widths

221

HOW TO ARC YOUR UPSTROKES

You'll certainly be utilising diagonal slopes when constructing your letters, and implementing arcs in place of diagonals will allow your letters to be recognised. Apart from being able to distinguish a connecting 'm–n' from an 'm–u', arcs give your letters organic characteristics that make them easier on the eyes.

Commmmicate   *Communicate*

Using diagonals for every upstroke creates letter blending, making the word difficult to read.

Arcs allow more harmony throughout your letterforms. The connecting northwest arcs will naturally run into the following letter at its waistline, differentiating the letters from one another.

Just like your diagonal upstroke, move your marker up using the tip, but this time—in an arcing motion. When moving upwards in a northwest direction, start with your thumb bent and gradually release so when you complete the upstroke, your thumb is fully extended.

For a northeasterly arc you'll want to use more of your wrist and hand to round your arcs. This motion is a bit more unnatural than the northwest movement, so allow your wrist to come into play. This will help compensate for the need to overextend your fingers. Use your index finger to help guide the marker in this direction with your wrist taking on the majority of the workload. When you complete the stroke, watch how your hand and forearm will lock into alignment with each other.

HOW TO ARC YOUR DOWNSTROKES

When making a thick arcing downstroke, you'll use the broad side of your marker and pull down—the same idea from the previous basic downstroke. However, instead of a straight diagonal, use increased pointer finger pressure and move your fingers in a semi-circular motion.

Let's start off by reviewing how to make a right-to-left arcing downstroke. To begin, rest the edge of your marker on your paper the same way you would make your initial diagonal downstroke. Instead of moving straight down, pull ever so slightly to the left while rounding your stroke and applying pressure using your fingers and wrist to make the shape. As soon as you begin to transition back to the right (about halfway between the midline and baseline), release pressure and swing upwards creating a thin exiting stroke.

The arcing left-to-right stroke will be the most difficult of all the basics covered thus far because it's the first time utilising both the upward and downward techniques in one continuous stroke.

Move edge slightly to the left, pull down and flick up

Arcing right-to-left downstroke compared to the arcing left-to-right downstroke. If you're doing it correctly, notice how the two strokes are able to rotate 180 degrees and replace one another by retaining their shape.

The arcing left-to-right stroke will be the most difficult of all the basics covered thus far because it's the first time utilising both the upward and downward techniques in one continuous stroke.

When starting off, use the northeast upward arcing stroke—but only partially since you'll be starting three quarters up from the baseline. As you peak just above the waistline, begin to turn your fingers inward and apply pressure. This pressure should be the most you apply out of any downstroke you've previously practised because the broad edge is going to be less generous as you move in back towards the left. As you transition downwards, taper the bottom by releasing pressure and pushing towards the left.

Two stroke method moving upward and transitioning downward.

HOW TO MAKE HORIZONTAL STROKE

You won't need to use horizontal lines nearly as much as your arcing and diagonal strokes, but they're necessary when completing certain letters like the arms of an 'E' or the crossbar of a 't'. You can use two different variations when making a horizontal stroke.

For a thin horizontal stroke, hold the marker the same way when applying an upstroke. Make sure your finger pressure is light and keep the marker upright. Lock your wrist and fingers in place so that their only job is to keep the marker steady in the same position. Move your arm either left-to-right or right-to-left making swift strokes. By locking your fingers and wrist, you take the shakiness out of play and you will be able to move quicker. Remember to go at a speed you're most comfortable with.

Now for thick horizontals, grip the marker like you would for a downstroke, but cock your wrist to the left so that you're able see every knuckle on your hand. Your pointer finger, wrist and forearm should all be aligned with one another and your marker should be wresting parallel to this line. In this position, you should be able to see the entire marker—including the point. Again, lock your fingers and wrist and move your arm in either direction and apply pressure. Remember to pause, then pull in either direction and pause to complete the stroke.

Move in either direction for thick and thin horizontals.

223

Hand-
lettering
Guide

CALLIGRAPHY BY
ANDREAS M HANSEN

Tool: Narrow Nib Ruling Pen

A B C D E F G
H I J K L M N
O P Q R S T
U V W X Y Z

Calligraphy by Andreas M Hansen

Calligraphy by Andreas M Hansen

CALLIGRAPHY BY
ANDREAS M HANSEN

abcdefg

hijklmn

opqrst

uvwxyz

e e e e e e e e e

f f f f f f f f f

g g g g g g g g g

h h h h h h h h h

i i i i i i i i i

j j j j j j j j j

Calligraphy by Andreas M Hansen

Calligraphy by Andreas M Hansen

Hand-
lettering
Guide

CALLIGRAPHY BY
HIDEYA MOTO

Tool: Hiro Leonardt 41 Calligraphy Nib

A B C D E F
G H I J K L M
N O P Q R S T
U V W X Y Z

a b c d e f g h i j k l
m n o p q r s t u
v w x y z

Calligraphy by HIDEYA MOTO

Calligraphy by HIDEYA MOTO

c *c c c c c c c c*

d *d d d d d d d*

e *e e e e e e e e*

f *f f f f f f f f*

g *g g g g g g g*

h *h h h h h h h h*

Calligraphy by HIDEYA MOTO

Calligraphy by HIDEYA MOTO

CALLIGRAPHY BY

SHARON TAN

Tool: Tombow ABT Dual Brush Pen

abcdefghijklm
nopqrstuvwxyz
ABCDEFGHI
JKLMNOPQR
STUVWXYZ

f f f f f f f f f f f f f f

g g g g g g g g g g g g g g

h h h h h h h h h h h h h h

i i i i i i i i i i i i i i

j j j j j j j j j j j j j j

k k k k k k k k k k k k k k

l l l l l l l l l l l l l l

Calligraphy by Sharon Tan

m

n

o

p

q

r

s

t

u

v

w

x

y

z

Calligraphy by Sharon Tan

Calligraphy by Sharon Tan

Calligraphy by Sharon Tan

CALLIGRAPHY BY
BENOIT BERGER
(SAY WHAT STUDIO)

Tool: Quill Pen, Automatic Pen

abcdefghijklmn
opqrstuvwxyz
ABCDEFGHI
JKLMNOPQR
STUVWXYZ

Calligraphy by Benoit Berger (Say What Studio)

Calligraphy by Benoit Berger (Say What Studio)

Calligraphy by Benoit Berger (Say What Studio)

Calligraphy by Benoit Berger (Say What Studio)

Calligraphy by Benoit Berger (Say What Studio)

Hand-
lettering
Guide

CALLIGRAPHY BY
COPENHAGEN SIGNS

Tool: Brush Pen

Calligraphy by Copenhagen Signs

Calligraphy by Copenhagen Signs

Calligraphy by Copenhagen Signs

CALLIGRAPHY BY
RIKI HARIMULYA

ABCDEFGH
IJKLMNOPQ
RSTUVWXYZ

abcdefghijklmn
opqrstuvwxyz

Step 1:
Outline your letter

Step 2:
Fill out the main voids

Step 3:
Stylise your letter

Calligraphy by Riki Harimulya

Calligraphy by Riki Harimulya

Calligraphy by Riki Harimulya

Calligraphy by Riki Harimulya

Calligraphy by Riki Harimulya

Abbey Sy / Adrian Iorga / Andreas M Hansen / Andreas Pedersen / Angi Phillips / Ben Johnston / Blaqk / CHALKBOY / Copenhagen Signs / Craig Black / David Sanden / Drew Melton / Edwin Shea Montero / ETLettering / Glenn Wolk / Hand Lettering Co. / HIDEYA MOTO / Igor Sturion / Inkdropletcreations / Isobel Hsu / Jimbo Bernaus / Jon Benson / Julia Razzhigaeva / Justin Poulter / Kamil Borowski / Katol @ Start from Zero / Mike Meyer / Neilson Letters / Niels Shoe Meulman / Nim Ben-Reuven / Northern Projects / Novia Jonatan / Olga Vasik / Paula Lee Calligraphy / Pragun Agarwal / Riki Harimulya / Rob Draper / RYLSEE / Say What Studio / Sharon Tan / Simon Walker / Swindler & Swindler / Tierney Studio / Tobias Saul / Tristan Kerr / TYRSA / Vlada Ruzhitskaya

AGARWAL, PRAGUN

P.116-117, 122-123

Graduated in graphic design from National Institute of Design, Agarwal is interested in illustration and design for print, and hand-lettering. He has three years of professional experience at brand consultant Codesign and Turmeric Design in India, his work has also been awarded in the illustration category at the Kyoorius Student Awards in 2014.

BEN-REUVEN, NIM

P.052-053, 110-111

A lettering artist, art director and video producer living in Brooklyn, New York, Ben-Reuven specialises in extremely elegant custom script lettering and extremely inelegant videos featuring himself as a cardboard robot failing at everything.

BENSON, JON

P.058, 170-171

Jon Benson is a graphic designer and illustrator living in Oklahoma. Benson discovered hand-lettering in 2014 and has drew inspiration from movies, songs, and clever quotes for his letterforms. His tools of the trade are a basic 0.7mm mechanical pencil, a Behance Dot Grid Book, Adobe Illustrator and Photoshop.

BERNAUS, JIMBO

P.156, 200-203

Jimbo Bernaus is an art director, visual designer and letterer from Barcelona, and founder of BAM! creative studio. His 6 years of experience in graphic design has connected him with global clients. His passions include travelling and meeting diverse creatives, who motivate him to become a better professional.

BLACK, CRAIG

P.149-150, 191

Craig is a Scottish-born graphic designer, lettering artist and typographer known for his typographic illustrations, visual identities, packaging, installations and murals. Craig believes in creating engaging, modern and precise visuals whilst maintaining originality in all of his work.

BLAQK

P.034-039, 134-136

Founded in 2011 in Athens, Blaqk is the collaboration between Greg Papagrigoriou and Chris Tzaferos, aka Simek. The duo works with murals, painting, graphic design, and more. Papagrigoriou works mostly with calligraphy while Simek with geometric shapes and lines. They participate in numerous exhibitions and festivals globally.

BOROWSKI, KAMIL

P.128-133

Started messing with letters since primary school, Borowski studied graphic design and painting at the Academy of Fine Arts in Lodz. His interest for fonts and typestyles has led him to calligraphy a few years later. It became a daily habit and Borowski writes on everything that is possible to write on.

CHALKBOY

P.010-015, 188-190

Started drawing on blackboards and doing chalk art while working at a café in Osaka, Japan, CHALKBOY found out how fun it was to draw with chalk during the process. He now travels worldwide to shops and cafes to draw on blackboards, and even extends his materials beyond chalk and blackboards to meet his clients' needs.

COPENHAGEN SIGNS

P.070-073

Founder of Copenhagen Signs is Jakob Engberg Petersen. With a background as a graphic designer, Petersen finished his sign technician apprenticeship in 2015 and began working with contemporary sign techniques, hand-lettering, typographic design and more. Petersen is also one of othe only full-time sign painters in Denmark.

DRAPER, ROB

P.182-187

UK-based artist and designer specialising in hand lettering, Draper has worked with a range of clients worldwide including GAP, Nike, Penguin Random House, Pentagram, Harper & Collins, and more. His work is featured in IdN, Design Taxi, Thames & Hudsons 'Typography' title, The Design Museum London, The Daily Mail, and other design blogs.

ETLETTERING

P.093

Founded in 2012 by Evgeny Tkhorzhevsky, a calligraphy and lettering artist and graphic designer from Vladivostok, Russia. ETLettering specialises in creating lettering and calligraphy logotypes. The team ignores all style restrictions in order to master in the full range of expressive possibilities of letter forms.

HAND LETTERING CO.

P.192-193

Chris Wright only took lettering seriously as a career until he got married. It started as a personal project to design a verse from the Bible every week, but through daily practice, his hand-lettering skills took shape and grew, which eventually led to him starting Hand Lettering Co.

HANSEN, ANDREAS M

P.124-127

Chris specialises in web design, art direction, calligraphy, and crafting brand identity. Also a self-taught calligraphist, Chris is known for his clean, minimalistic approach to the art form as well as his high-contrast aesthetic. Currently based in Copenhagen, Hansen has lived and worked around the world, most recently in Hong Kong.

HARIMULYA, RIKI

P.166-169

An art director at Agency Studio in Jakarta, Harimulya also draws custom types and illustrations.

HSU, ISOBEL

P.100-103

Isobel Hsu is a graphic designer who got into hand lettering and calligraphy after she had her baby boy three years ago. She likes to experiment with flourishes and try to come up with as many ideas as she can.

INKDROPLETCREATIONS

P.080-081, 086

ThInkdropletcreations AKA Evelyn Wong started practising calligraphy in 2015. Calligraphy has become a therapeutic practic for Evelyn, separating her mind like yoga from the hustling city life. She hopes to inspire people to pick up the art of both calligraphy and writing, since its beauty has been overshadowed by the convenience of technology today.

IORGA, ADRIAN

WP.075, 120, 165, 198-199

An independent graphic designer currently working from Bucharest, Romania, collaborating with people and companies from all around the globe, Iorga specialises in logo and brand identity design and have a great passion for typography and hand lettering. Iorga's work constantly blends and influences each other to give every project unique accents and distinctive personality.

JOHNSTON, BEN

P.108-109, 212-213

A self-taught designer who grew up in Cape Town, South Africa. After a brief stint in industrial design, Johnston started focusing on traditional graphic design, with a preference for creating typographic illustrations from scratch. His industrial design experience helps to break the confines of 2D and 3D, enabling him to bring his designs to life.

JONATAN, NOVIA

P.064, 077, 194-197

One stroke at a time is how Jonatan crafts letters.

KATOL / START FROM ZERO

P.040-045

A member of Start From Zero, Katol specialises in handwritten lettering signboard. Graduated from the Hong Kong Polytechnic University School of Design, Katol worked with Commerical Radio Productions, I.T. and more, creating graphic design and visual arts while building his own concept store and clothing label Rat's Cave.

KERR, TRISTAN

P.214-215

After working as a print technician and designer for several years, Tristan discovered his passion for typography, urban art and hand sign-painting. His commissions span from hand-painted advertisements and urban art murals and illustrations for renowned brands. Based in Australia, his work has been exhibited in galleries throughout Australia and Europe.

MELTON, DREW

P.059-061, 087-089

Melton is a freelance graphic designer, letterer and occasional illustrator. He has worked for a wide range of clients including Nike, Harrods and Penguin Books. He currently resides in New Orleans with his beautiful wife and stacks of paper.

MEULMAN, NIELS SHOE

P.028-033

Being a graffiti pioneer from Amsterdam, Meulman worked with New York counterparts like Dondi White, Rammellzee and Keith Haring in the 1980s. Experimenting within the traditional medium of paint-on-canvas, Meulman revolutionised the art of writing when he initiated the calligraffiti movement. Meulman is now represented by Galerie Gabriel Rolt, Amsterdam and Galerie Droste, Wuppertal.

MEYER, MIKE

P.208-211

A sign painter from Minnesota, Meyer has run his own business since 1989 and travels the world to host and support letterheads sign painter events. He is an ambassador for the sign painting business and was featured in the Sign Painters, the film. Meyer held his first workshop in Christchurch, which inspired people across three continents.

MONTERO, EDWIN SHEA
P.208-211

A passionate graphic designer from NYC with a Bachelor of Fine Arts in Graphic Design, Edwin Shea Montero works freelance within medias from print to apparel to web-design to calligraphy. His hobbies include hand lettering short motivational quotes that Montero finds inspiring in his everyday life.

MOTO, HIDEYA
P.112-115, 236-245

Moto Lettering AKA Hideya Moto is a Japanese freelance calligrapher who works with tools like dip pens, brush pens, Apple Pencil, pencils and chalk. He began learning calligraphy online in 2015, and now does logo designs, and calligraphy for events, workshops, lessons, mural paintings and more.

NEILSON LETTERS
P. 096-099

Neilson Letters Calligraphy & Engraving is based in Montreal and services worldwide. Owner Erin Neilson is well-versed in paper-related etiquette with a background in custom printing. She uses calligraphy and engraving to create a bespoke experience for her clients, namely CHANEL, Louis Vuitton and MaxMara.

NORTHERN PROJECTS
P.208-211

The studio of lettering and graphic designer Laura Dillema. With a background of graphic design, Laura became interested in hand-lettering after graduation, which prompted her to create her own unique, self-taught style. She has worked with brands all over the world, striving for authenticity, originality and genuine craftsmanship in every design.

PAULA LEE CALLIGRAPHY
P.094-095

A creative studio specialising in calligraphy services and custom stationery for weddings and special events. Inspired by nature, Paula creates work that is delicate, refined and simple. She is passionate about bringing unique personality to wedding stationery, paper goods, brand identities and anything else that can be written on.

PEDERSEN, ANDREAS
P.162-164

Letterer, illustrator and all-round graphical radness creator from Sweden, Pedersen has a great variety of interests. Graduated in Design and Visual Communication from Linnaeus University in 2015 and received a certificate for Interactive Art Direction from Hyper Island in 2016.

PHILLIPS, ANGI
P.022-027

Angelique Ink AKA Angi is a calligraphy artist, specialising in a range of handwritten calligraphy and custom script designs. She creates original custom script designs for branding, products and events, murals and licensed artwork. Angi teaches workshops on modern calligraphy, sharing her passion with students all over the world.

POULTER, JUSTIN
P.178-181

The commercial illustrator and lettering artist landed his first job for an award-winning studio in London. Poulter went freelance in 2014 and has worked for international clients including National Geographic, Google, Vans, Nike, Coca Cola, etc.

RAZZHIGAEVA, JULIA
P.082-085

Julia Razzhigaeva lives in Vladivostok, and has created calligraphy since 2018 with a focus on Copperplate script. She is a member of the IAMPETH (the International Association of Master Penmen, Engrossers and Teachers of Handwriting). She also wrote a manual about copperplate flourishes in 2020.

RUZHITSKAYA, VLADA
P.138-143

Vlada Ruzhitskaya AKA rvvlada is a Moscow-based calligrapher with a passion for lettering and calligraphy. Previously an illustrator, she took interest in font design and found a passion for Slavic culture and folk art, where she is an expert in Old Slavic style writing known as Vyaz.

RYLSEE
P.016-021

RYLSEE aka Cyril Vouilloz is an visual artist originally from Geneva currently living in Berlin. With a background in typography, design and mural painting, RYLSEE has worked for local and international companies on branding, promotion, and in-store display installations around the world, and also co-created a clothing label, SNEEER.com with his brother.

SANDEN, DAVID
P.074, 092

David studied graphic design in Spain and lives between Valencia and London. He freelances besides personal projects on screenprinting, typography and lettering exploration, font design, illustration and photography. Influenced by 80s skateboarding aesthetic, punk culture, 60's psychedelia and rock art posters, Sanden always try to stick to the old school way, rather than just vector flat clean design.

SAUL, TOBIAS
P.048-051, 090-091

Tobias is a lettering artist and graphic designer from Düsseldorf, Germany. His experience in graffiti and illustration helped him develop a feeling for letters and layouts before his study of communication design, where he developed a great passion for lettering and illustration. His major fields include logo, branding and packaging design.

SAY WHAT STUDIO
P.062-063, 151-152

A graphic design studio based in Paris running by Benoit Berger and Nathalie Kapagiannidi. Bound by a common passion, the pair founded Say What Studio after graduating from the ECV school in 2011.

STURION, IGOR
P.137, 144-145

Igor is an art director and calligrapher interested in all things visual. Sturion tries to find the fine edge between art and design, as sorting things within categories creates limits in achieving true potential. Nothing excites Sturion more than a job or an art piece that will cross these lines.

SWINDLER & SWINDLER
P.054-057, 076-079

Created in 2015 by two French illustrators based in Grenoble, France. On one side is rigor, precision and control brought to you by Mr. and his type work, where the Mrs. brings smoothness and poetry in her ornamental work. Separate and complementary, these two graphic worlds meet at last and produce thorough compositions under Swindler & Swindler.

SY, ABBEY
P.204-206

An artist and author based in Manila, Philippines, who specialises in hand lettering and travel illustration. Working as a creative entrepreneur, Abbey freelances while producing her own merchandise, and has also written best-selling books on lettering and journaling. Her work is featured in a local and international scale.

TAN, SHARON
P.104-107

A calligrapher as well as hand-letter and journaling enthusiast from Kuala Lumpur, Malaysia. Sharon's style is flowy and airy together with whimsical watercolour illustrations such as simple wreaths and florals.

TIERNEY STUDIO
P.118-119, 216

The work place of Colin Tierney specialising in hand lettering, calligraphy and branding.

TYRSA
P.157-161

The Paris-based hand-drawn type master went from graffiti artist to graphic designer, where he carved a career for himself with a passion for hand-crafted typography. Now working on print and digital commissions, Tyrsa delivers polished, highly appealing digital and handmade work ranging from murals, posters, and enormous installations to small, detailed packaging designs.

VASIK, OLGA
P.068-069, 153, 207

Lettering artist and designer currently based in Chelyabinsk, Russia. In her work, Vasik pays the most attention to letterforms construction, relationships between the letters and counter forms of the letters. Her lettering style is influenced by the 60's rock music, extreme sports and US yellow pages advertising.

WALKER, SIMON
P.154-155

Walker is a freelance designer and custom-typographer working in Austin, Texas. Some of his clients, past and present, include Nickelodeon, American Eagle, Ed Helms, Vanity Fair, Pepsi, ESPN, Brené Brown, Nike and Target.

WOLK, GLENN
P.063-065, 148-153

Growing up with passion for fine art, Glenn studied graphic design and gained technical skills which helped him combine graphic design and typography with painting. He also received an Masters Degree in Fine Art later on. For Glenn, computers are a secondary creative tool while drawing remains the primary.

ACKNOWLEDGEMENTS

We would like to thank all the designers and companies who have involved in the production of this
book. This project would not have been accom-
plished without their significant contribution to
the compilation of this book. We would also like to
express our gratitude to all the producers for their
invaluable opinions and assistance throughout
this entire project. The successful completion
also owes a great deal to many professionals in
the creative industry who have given us precious
insights and comments. And to the many others
whose names are not credited but have made
specific input in this book, we thank you for your
continuous support the whole time.

FUTURE EDITIONS

If you wish to participate in viction:ary's future
projects and publications, please send your web-
site or portfolio to submit@victionary.com